men who do sexy

sexy

/ˈsɛksi/

adjective

1. 1.

sexually attractive or exciting.

"sexy French underwear"

synonyms:

sexually attractive, seductive, desirable, alluring, inviting, sensual, sultry, slinky, provocative, tempting, tantalizing; More

•

1. 2.

INFORMAL

very exciting or appealing.

"business magazines might not seem like the sexiest career choice"

synonyms:

exciting, stimulating, interesting, appealing, intriguing;

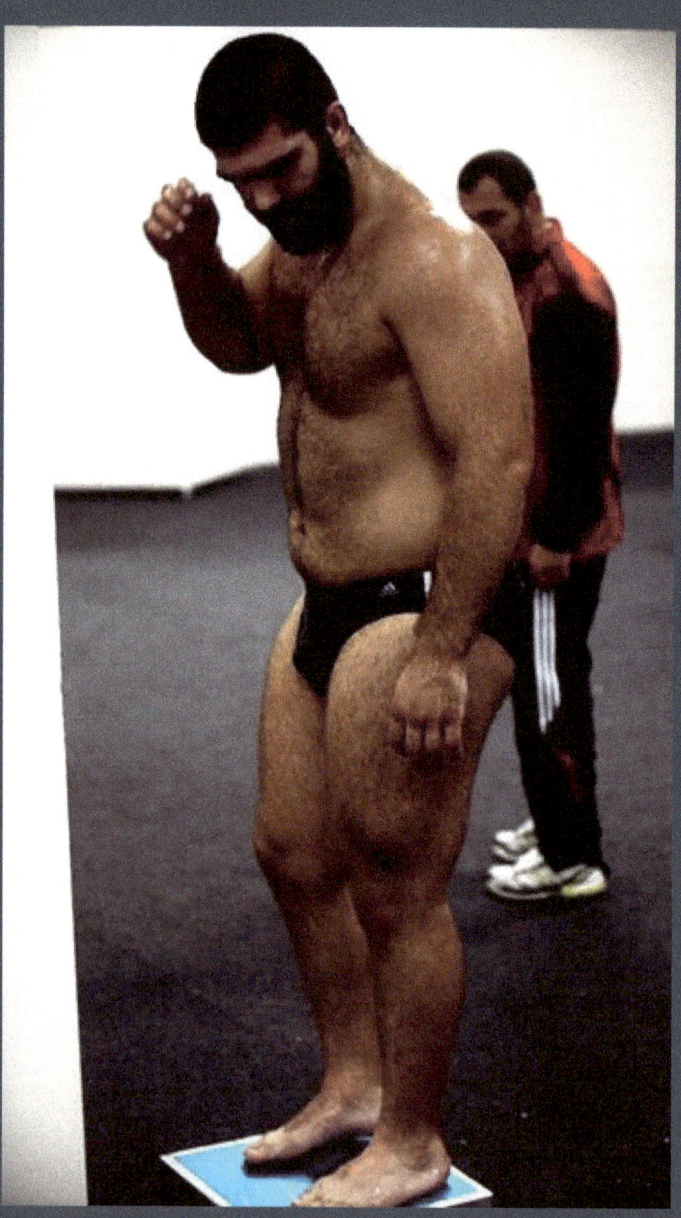

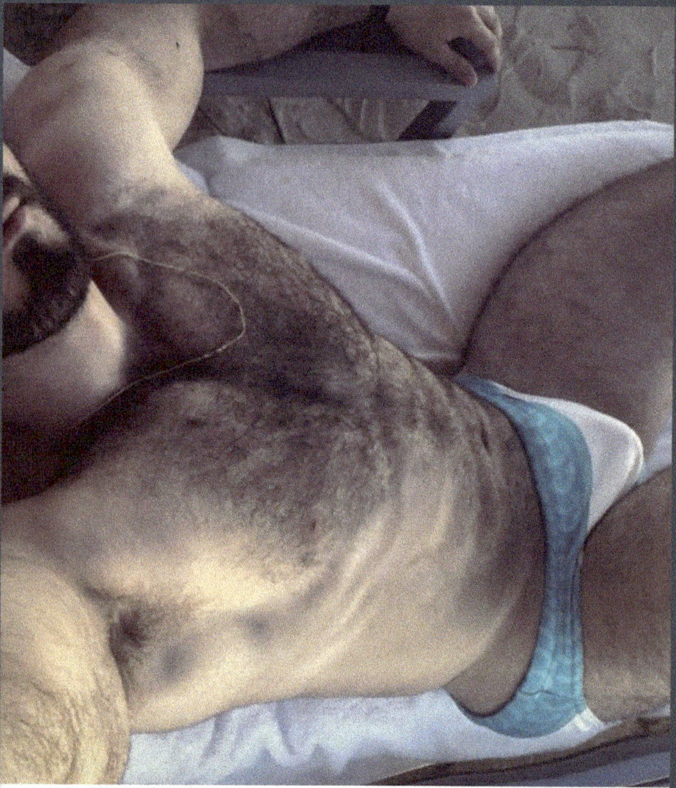

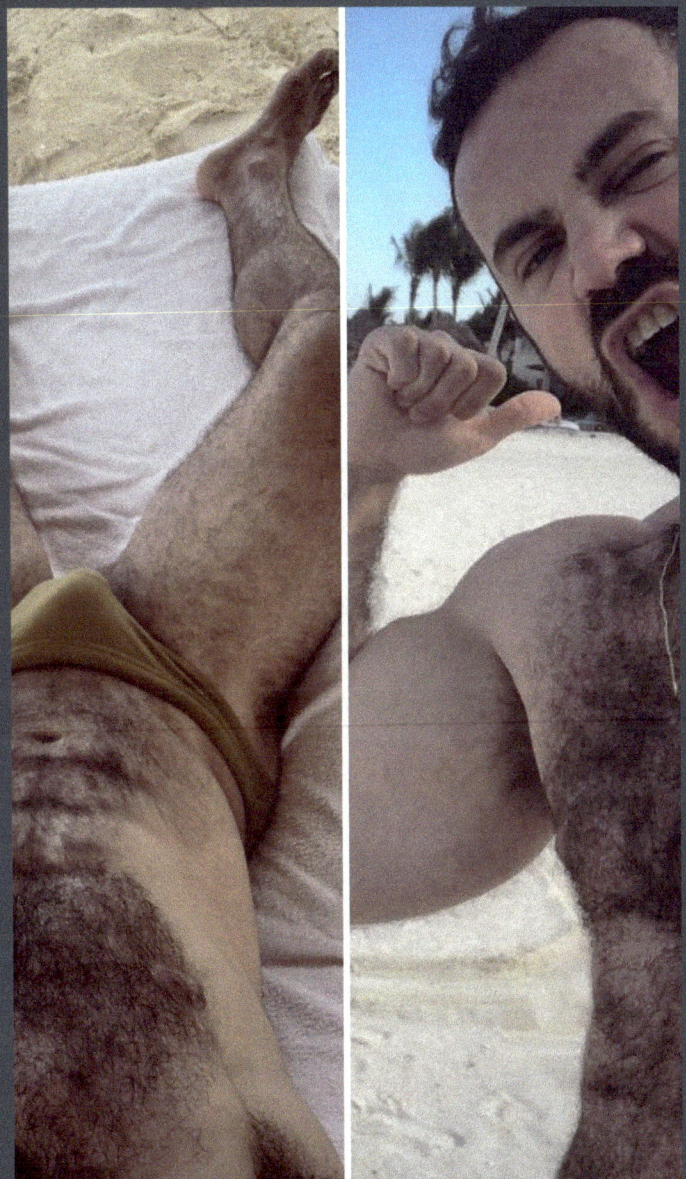

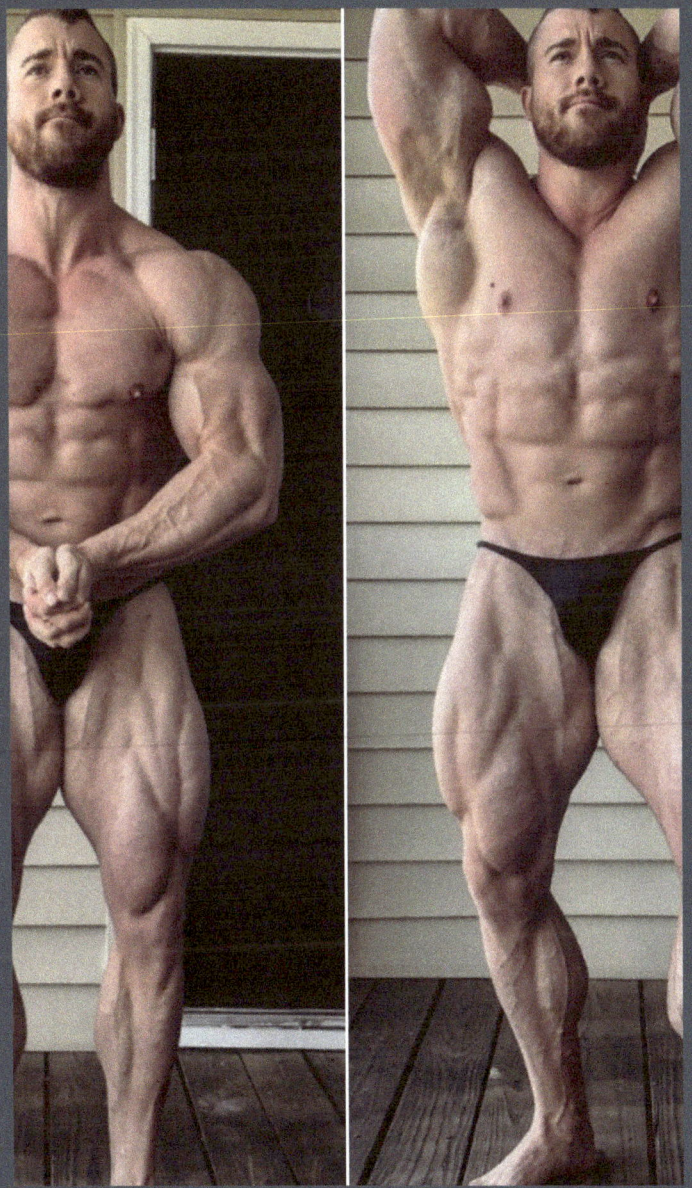

Svakim danom sve
veći i veći

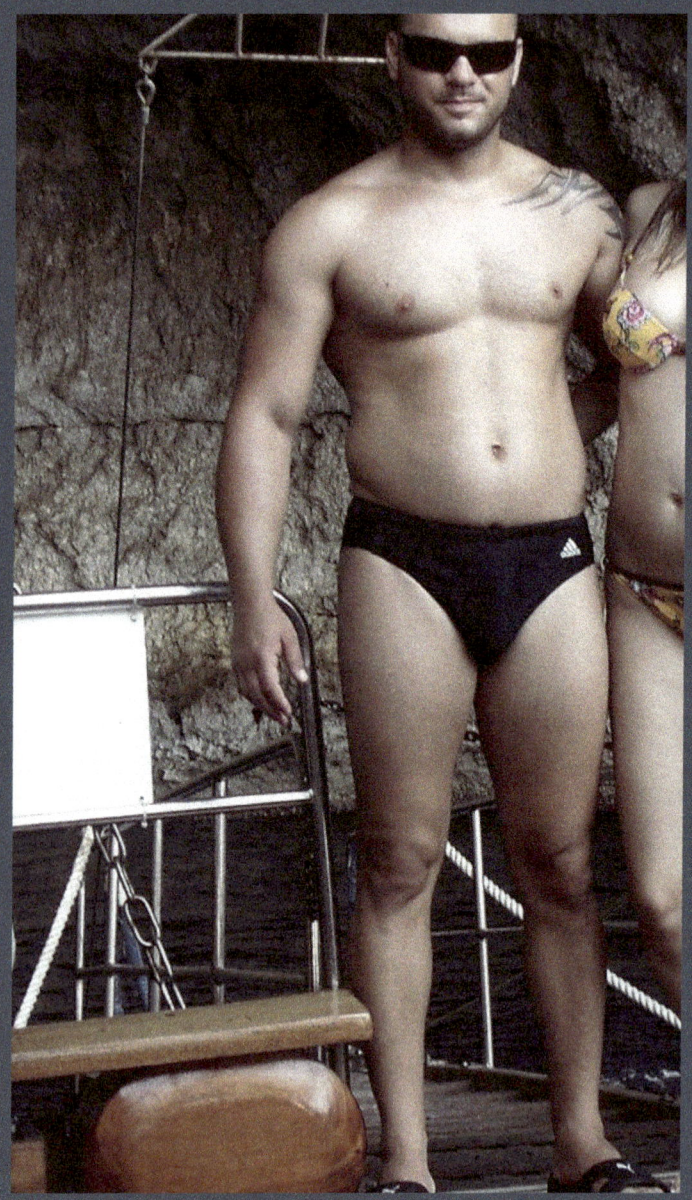

CPSIA information can be obtained
at www.ICGtesting.com
Printed in the USA
BVHW022100070419
544723BV00026B/61/P

9 780368 500435